The Seven Continents

North America

KAREN KELLAHER

Children's Press®
An Imprint of Scholastic Inc.

Content Consultant

Edwin A. Martini, Ph.D., Professor of History, Western Michigan University

Library of Congress Cataloging-in-Publication Data
Names: Kellaher, Karen, author.
Title: North America / by Karen Kellaher.
Description: New York, NY : Children's Press, 2019. | Series: A true book | Includes bibliographical
   references and index.
Identifiers: LCCN 2018021702| ISBN 9780531128091 (library binding) | ISBN 9780531134177 (pbk.)
Subjects: LCSH: North America—Juvenile literature.
Classification: LCC E38.5 .K45 2019 | DDC 970—dc23
LC record available at https://lccn.loc.gov/2018021702

All rights reserved. Published in 2019 by Children's Press, an imprint of Scholastic Inc.
Printed in North Mankato, MN, USA 113

SCHOLASTIC, CHILDREN'S PRESS, A TRUE BOOK™, and associated logos are trademarks and/or
registered trademarks of Scholastic Inc.

Scholastic Inc., 557 Broadway, New York, NY 10012

1 2 3 4 5 6 7 8 9 10 R 28 27 26 25 24 23 22 21 20 19

Front: North America
Back: Bison

Find the Truth!

Everything you are about to read is true *except* for one of the sentences on this page.

Which one is **TRUE**?

T or F Christopher Columbus was the first person from Europe to land in North America.

T or F In the northernmost parts of North America, no trees grow.

Find the answers in this book.

3

Contents

THE BIG TRUTH!

Major Meltdown

Tree frog

Bison

California condor

ASIA

ARCTIC
OCEAN

Ellesmere I.

ICELAND (Europe)

Greenland
(DENMARK)

Beaufort
Sea

Bering Strait

Alaska (U.S.)

Baffin
Bay

Yukon River

Baffin I.

Mackenzie River

Arctic Circle

Labrador
Sea

Aleutian
Islands

Kodiak I.

Gulf of
Alaska

Great Bear Lake

Great Slave Lake

Graham I.

Hudson
Bay

Newfoundland

Vancouver I.

CANADA

Columbia River

L. Superior

Ottawa

Nova Scotia

ATLANTIC
OCEAN

PACIFIC
OCEAN

Great Salt Lake

Missouri River

L. Huron

L. Michigan

L. Ontario

Cape Cod
Nantucket I.

L. Erie

Long I.

Washington, D.C.

UNITED STATES

Ohio River

Bermuda (U.K.)

Mississippi River

← 2,500 MI

Turks & Caicos (U.K.)

Hawaii (U.S.)

BAHAMAS

DOMINICAN
REPUBLIC

Anguilla (U.

PACIFIC
OCEAN

MEXICO

Gulf of Mexico

CUBA

British
Virgin Is.

Puerto
Rico
(U.S.)

ST. K
& NI

ANT
& BA

Guade

Revillagigedo Is. (Mexico)

Mexico
City

Cancun

JAMAICA

U.S. Virgin Is.

HAITI

Montserrat (U.K.)

DO

BELIZE

Martinique (Fr.)

S

HONDURAS

ST. VINCENT &
THE GRENADINES

B

Central
America

Caribbean Sea

GRENADA

GUATEMALA

EL SALVADOR

Panama
Canal

N

SOUTH
AMERICA

W   E

0   300 MI

NICARAGUA

S

0   500 KM

COSTA RICA

PANAMA

6

Continent Close-up

North America is the third-largest

Ottawa, Canada

of Earth's seven continents. It stretches from the icy Arctic region in the north to tropical Panama in the south. The top of North America is very wide. But the bottom is a narrow strip of land that links North America to South America. At its narrowest, it measures only 30 miles (48 kilometers) across! North America includes Canada, the United States, Mexico, and seven small countries in Central America. Many islands are also part of the continent.

Saint Kitts

Land area	9.4 million square miles (24 million sq km)
Number of independent countries	23
Estimated population (2017)	579 million
Main languages	English, Spanish, French
Largest country	Canada
Smallest country	Saint Kitts and Nevis
Fast fact	Hawaii is a state in the United States, but it is technically not part of North America. Its islands are usually counted as part of the Oceania region.

Death Valley can sometimes go more than a year without receiving any rain.

Death Valley, California, is the hottest and driest spot on the whole continent.

CHAPTER 1

Land and Climate

Long ago, large parts of North America were covered in glaciers. As these giant ice sheets moved and melted, they helped shape the land. Today, North America has one of the most varied landscapes in the world. It has many different **climate** zones, too. In the far north, temperatures are below freezing for most of the year. But in southern parts of the continent, it can get so hot that people burn their feet if they try to walk barefoot.

Highs and Lows

Many tall mountain ranges tower over western North America. The largest is the Rocky Mountains. The Rockies extend for about 3,000 miles (4,828 km) across the western parts of Canada and the United States. Other big ranges in this region are Mexico's Sierra Madre and the Alaska Range.

Much of eastern North America is hilly, too. The Appalachian Mountains run from Canada to the southeastern United States. The Appalachians are older and lower than the mountain ranges in the west.

Denali, a mountain in the Alaska Range, is the continent's highest peak. It is 20,310 feet (6,190 meters) tall.

The Canadian Shield in eastern Canada is a rocky plateau, or raised area that is flat. It contains some of the oldest rock in the world. The middle of North America is known for its gently rolling plains. This area has rich soil that is perfect for growing crops. The soil was created millions of years ago when the glaciers melted. Water flowed across the land, leaving tiny bits of rock, clay, and sand behind.

NORTH AMERICA'S TERRAIN

ARCTIC OCEAN

Greenland Ice Sheet

Alaska Range
Denali

Arctic Circle

Gulf of Alaska

Rocky Mountains

Hudson Bay

Canadian Shield

PACIFIC OCEAN

Mt. Whitney

Great Plains

Appalachian Mtns.

ATLANTIC OCEAN

Sierra Madre

Gulf of Mexico

Caribbean Sea

SOUTH AMERICA

KEY
TERRAIN
Ice   Mountains   Hills   Lowlands

This map shows where North America's higher and lower areas are.

Waterways

North America is bordered by the Arctic Ocean to the north, the Pacific Ocean to the west, and the Atlantic Ocean to the east. The Gulf of Mexico is a section of the Atlantic Ocean that juts into North America. Both the United States and Mexico have land surrounding the Gulf of Mexico. The Caribbean Sea is also considered part of the Atlantic. It is dotted with thousands of small islands and a handful of larger ones.

Like many places in the Caribbean Sea, the islands of St. Vincent and the Grenadines feature beautiful, sandy beaches.

A whopping 3,160 tons (2,866,704 kilograms) of water flows over Niagara Falls every second.

North America has millions of lakes and rivers. The five Great Lakes—Superior, Michigan, Huron, Erie, and Ontario—are located on or near the U.S.-Canada border. Together, they contain the planet's largest collection of freshwater. Water from four of the lakes drains into the Niagara River and later flows over the famous Niagara Falls. The continent's longest rivers are the mighty Mississippi and the Missouri. They flow through the middle of the United States and meet in the state of Missouri.

Climate

Because of the path Earth travels around the sun, the top of North America gets little direct sunlight. Summers there are short. Winters are long and icy cold. But the southern parts of the continent are close to Earth's **equator**. The sun shines directly on these areas, so it's hot all year long. Most places lie between these extremes. They have **temperate** climates with changing seasons.

Some parts of the continent get as much as 260 inches (660 centimeters) of rainfall each year. But dry areas such as California's Death Valley can get less than 3 inches (7.6 cm).

RECORD TEMPERATURES

HIGHEST	LOWEST
Death Valley, California, United States; July 1913	Yukon Territory, Canada; February 1947
134°F	-81.4°F
56.7°C	-63°C

Located in northwestern Canada, near Alaska, the Yukon region experiences tremendously cold winters.

The Grand Canyon

One of North America's most breathtaking sights is the Grand Canyon. This natural wonder is located in Arizona in the southwestern United States. It is 277 miles (446 km) long, up to 18 miles (29 km) wide, and more than 1 mile (1.6 km) deep! The rocky canyon was carved long ago by the Colorado River. Over millions of years, the rushing river wore away the rock around it. Today, the river still flows through the bottom of the canyon.

About five million people visit the Grand Canyon every year. Some even hike all the way to the bottom!

The Grand Canyon became a U.S. national park in 1919.

15

Elf owls often make their homes in the cacti of desert areas in northern Mexico and the southwestern United States.

The elf owl is one of the world's smallest owl species.

CHAPTER 2

Plants and Animals

Picture a green, leafy forest full of deer or a scorching desert where birds cool off inside cactus plants. These are two of North America's many amazing biomes. A biome is a natural area known for a certain climate, landscape, and living things. North America's biomes make ideal homes for thousands of plant and animal species. Each biome's native species have special traits that help them survive the conditions in their environment.

Northern Biomes

At the top of North America is the icy **tundra**. This biome is so cold that the soil stays frozen all year. No trees grow there, but small plants like mosses and grasses survive. Wildflowers bloom during the short summer. Tundra animals have many tricks for staying warm. Polar bears have a thick layer of fat, while birds migrate south for the winter.

South of the tundra is an area called the boreal forest, or taiga. This chilly biome is made up of evergreen trees like spruces and pines. Many mammals there grow thick winter coats.

Wildflowers and other plants that are low to the ground grow in the tundra of northwestern Canada.

Arctic foxes have thick fur to keep them warm in the far northern parts of the continent.

Changing Forests

North America's temperate **deciduous** forests have trees with leaves that change color and fall off each autumn. New leaves grow in spring. These forests are the

ARCTIC OCEAN

Arctic Circle

Gulf of Alaska

Hudson Bay

PACIFIC OCEAN

ATLANTIC OCEAN

BIOMES
- High mountain
- Tundra
- Taiga
- Temperate forest
- Grassland
- Savanna
- Tropical rain forest
- Desert
- Fresh water
- Ice

Gulf of Mexico

Caribbean Sea

SOUTH AMERICA

perfect home for many kinds of wildlife, from insects and turtles to white-tailed deer. These animals must cope with the changing seasons. Some, such as black bears and skunks, **hibernate** during the colder months.

Enormous bison graze on grass in Yellowstone National Park.

At Home on the Prairie

Much of the middle of North America is made up of prairie land. The most important plants in this biome are grasses. These grasses have deep roots and are hardy enough to survive the changing seasons. Plant-eating mammals such as deer and pronghorns graze on them. Other common prairie animals include **predators** such as coyotes, foxes, and hawks. Some smaller animals, such as prairie dogs, dig underground burrows that help them hide from these hunters.

Desert Life

The United States and Mexico both have large sections of desert. This biome typically receives less than 10 inches (25 cm) of rainfall a year and can be scorching hot, but plants and animals have all sorts of survival tricks. The barrel cactus has a special shape that allows it to expand as it soaks up rainwater. This lets it store water during dry periods. Many desert animals, including snakes, bats, and jackrabbits, are active mainly at night. This helps them avoid the daytime heat.

The coloring and texture of a horned lizard's skin help it blend in with desert environments.

All Wet

Tropical rain forests cover parts of southern Mexico, Central America, and the Caribbean. They are warm all year and get up to 260 inches (660 cm) of rain. Sloths and parrots hang out in the treetops. The continent's largest cat— the jaguar—roams the forest floor. The northern Pacific coastline has temperate rain forests. These areas are cooler than a tropical rain forest and receive less rain. They have cedar and hemlock trees, black bears, squirrels, and salamanders.

North America also has aquatic biomes. Many species make their homes in the continent's lakes and rivers and in the oceans along its coasts.

Red-eyed tree frogs live among the trees of Central American rain forests. They rarely come down to the ground.

Species in Trouble

Many of North America's plant and animal species are in danger of dying out, usually due to human activities. Here are just a few:

Red Wolf

Home: Eastern United States

Red wolves nearly died out because of hunting and habitat loss.

California Condor

Home: Southwestern United States and northern Mexico

People used to shoot these huge birds. Habitat loss also continues to be a problem.

Staghorn Coral

Home: Coasts of Florida, Mexico, the Bahamas, and some Caribbean islands

Corals are collections of tiny animals called coral polyps. They are being killed by pollution and rising water temperatures.

Ash Tree

Home: Mainly eastern and central North America

These trees are being killed by emerald ash borers, insects that were accidentally brought to North America from Asia.

Black-footed Ferret

Home: Central North America from southern Canada to northern Mexico

These furry mammals are threatened by habitat loss, disease, and dwindling food sources. At one point, experts feared they were already extinct.

Kemp's Ridley Sea Turtle

Home: Gulf of Mexico and Atlantic Ocean

These turtles get tangled in fishing gear, and they face the dangers of pollution and habitat loss. People used to eat their eggs in large numbers.

Major Meltdown

North America has more land inside the Arctic Circle than any other continent. The Arctic Circle is an area of land that borders the Arctic Ocean. It is covered in ice for much of the year. But there is a problem. Earth's average temperature has been slowly rising. This warm-up is causing more and more Arctic sea ice to melt each summer. This diagram shows how this process takes place.

3 Water soaks up heat from the sun better than ice does. So now the ocean gets even warmer.

2 Ice in the ocean melts and shrinks.

4 More ice melts.

1 Air and ocean temperatures rise. Scientists say one cause is the burning of oil and other fossil fuels to power cars and factories. This creates gases that trap the sun's heat close to Earth.

5 The cycle continues. Over time, there is less space for animals, such as polar bears and walruses, which live on large chunks of ice. Higher ocean levels can also cause flooding in coastal areas around the world.

These cliff homes in the southwestern United States were built by Ancestral Pueblo people about 800 years ago.

Colorado's Mesa Verde National Park is home to more than 600 Ancestral Pueblo cliff dwellings.

CHAPTER 3

A Peek at the Past

The first humans in North America came from Asia sometime around 12,000 BCE. The exact details of their journey remain a mystery. Experts have long believed that the travelers walked across a land bridge that once connected Asia to Alaska, then walked deeper into North America. Now some scholars have a new idea. They think that some of the travelers may have taken boats. However the travelers arrived, their descendants spread out across the continent. They were the first Native Americans.

Native North Americans

By the 1400s, millions of people lived in North America. They belonged to hundreds of cultures with different customs and languages. Some groups, like the Chipewyan of Canada, were mostly **nomadic**. They traveled around for much of the year hunting for food. Others, like the Iroquois of the northeastern United States, settled in one place. They planted crops and set up villages. Sometimes, neighboring groups cooperated and traded with one another. In other cases, they had frequent conflicts.

Two of the continent's most advanced native civilizations were the Maya and the Aztecs. The Maya lived in what is now Mexico and Central America starting about 4,000 years ago. The Aztecs made

MAJOR NATIVE AMERICAN GROUPS, AROUND 1500

Note: Not all Native North American groups are labeled on map.

their home in Mexico starting about 800 years ago. Both cultures developed sprawling empires with great cities. They created their own calendars and systems of writing. The Maya wrote books on paper made from tree bark.

Newcomers Arrive

About a thousand years ago, people from Europe
began making their way to North America. The first
to arrive were the Vikings from Norway, who visited
Canada around the year 1000. In 1492, Christopher
Columbus made his famous journey from Spain. He
explored islands off North America's coast. But he
thought he had landed in the Indies, a part of Asia.
So he called the native people Indians.

North America's Timeline

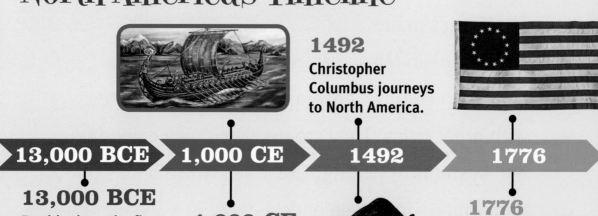

1492
Christopher
Columbus journeys
to North America.

| 13,000 BCE | 1,000 CE | 1492 | 1776 |

13,000 BCE
By this time, the first
people have arrived
in North America.

1,000 CE
The Vikings sail
to Canada.

1776
The United States
becomes the
continent's first
independent country

Soon, many people from Europe settled in North America and set up **colonies**. But not everyone came freely. Hundreds of thousands of Africans were brought to North America as slaves. They were forced to work on farms.

The Europeans' arrival meant big changes for Native Americans. Settlers took their land and introduced diseases that native people had never encountered. Many Native Americans died.

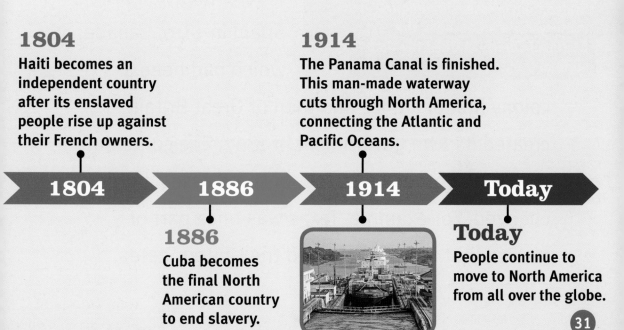

1804
Haiti becomes an independent country after its enslaved people rise up against their French owners.

1914
The Panama Canal is finished. This man-made waterway cuts through North America, connecting the Atlantic and Pacific Oceans.

1804 > 1886 > 1914 > Today

1886
Cuba becomes the final North American country to end slavery.

Today
People continue to move to North America from all over the globe.

Many people moved to the United States from overseas in the 20th century. For a lot of them, the Statue of Liberty marked the first sight of their new home.

Time of Change

Over time, most European colonies in North America won their independence. The United States broke away from Great Britain in 1776. Mexico declared its independence from Spain in 1810. Canada, which had been a colony first of France and then of Great Britain, created its own government in 1867. The continent changed in other ways, too. In some cases, borders changed. For example, Texas was once part of Mexico, but in 1845, it joined the United States.

A Letter From Columbus

Christopher Columbus wrote this letter in 1493 to tell Spain's king about his first trip to North America.

I know that it will please you to learn that my voyage has been a success. I am writing to tell you about the discoveries I have made. Thirty-three days after I departed from Cadiz, Spain, I reached the Indian sea, where I found many islands. Many men were living there. I claimed these islands for our great king by making a proclamation and flying our flags. No one tried to stop us. . . . When I sent men to the villages to speak with the natives, the natives ran off as my men approached.

Columbus had really reached the Caribbean Sea in North America.

THINK ABOUT IT:
Why do you think Native Americans ran away when Columbus's men approached?

Columbus said the islands now belonged to Spain.

Christopher Columbus lands on the shores of El Salvador in 1492.

The letter has been adapted and shortened for young readers.
Source: Gilder Lehrman Institute of American History.

More than 8.6 million people live in New York City.

North America's two biggest cities by population are Mexico City in Mexico and New York City (pictured) in the United States.

34

CHAPTER 4

North America Today

Today, North America's 579 million people live in 23 independent nations and more than a dozen territories that are controlled by foreign countries. They speak hundreds of different languages. While some North Americans make their homes in the countryside, about 80 percent of the population lives in and around cities. That's a higher percentage than any other continent.

Diverse People

There are still large numbers of Native Americans in some parts of North America. For example, in southern Mexico and Central America, millions of people are of Maya descent. In other parts of the continent, most people are descended from Europeans, Africans, and other groups. And the face of the continent is still changing. People from all over the world still **immigrate** to North America, especially to the United States.

People offer goods for sale at an outdoor market in a small town in Guatemala.

Parliament Hill in the capital city of Ottawa serves as the meeting place for Canada's lawmakers.

Who's in Charge?

Most of North America's countries have democratic governments where people elect their leaders. The United States and Mexico are two examples. In those nations, citizens vote for both a president and a group of leaders who make the laws. Canada is a democracy, too, but it works a little differently. People there elect members of a lawmaking group called the parliament. The head of the biggest political party in parliament becomes the nation's prime minister.

A farm worker shows off freshly picked coffee beans at a Costa Rican farm.

Economy

The United States and Canada have many natural resources, including oil and natural gas. Their factories make thousands of different products, and their farms supply much of the world's wheat and corn. Many people live comfortably.

Other nations are not as well off. Mexico's economy has been growing quickly in recent years, but almost half of its people still live in poverty. Poverty is also high in Central America and on some Caribbean islands. Many people in those areas work on farms. Others are employed in the tourism industry.

Made in North America

An export is a product that a country sells to other nations. This graph shows the top export for each of North America's four biggest countries. The United States, Canada, and Mexico send much of their exports to each other. For example, most U.S. oil is sold to Canada and Mexico.

Top Export by Country

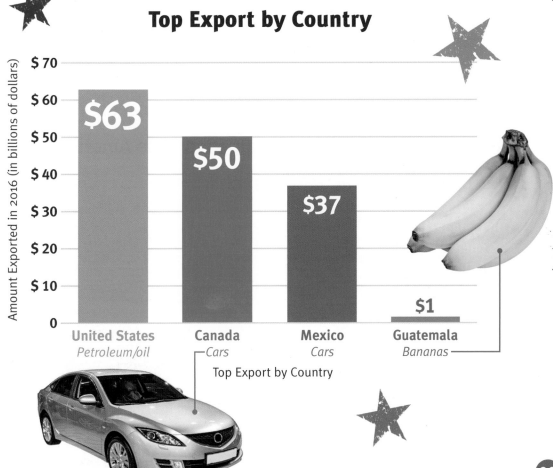

Amount Exported in 2016 (in billions of dollars)

- $70
- $60
- $50
- $40
- $30
- $20
- $10
- 0

United States	Canada	Mexico	Guatemala
$63	$50	$37	$1
Petroleum/oil	Cars	Cars	Bananas

Top Export by Country

Source: MIT Observatory of Economic Complexity

Food and Sport

Some of North America's favorite foods have a long history on the continent. For example, many early Native Americans grew corn. Today, corn tortillas are a staple in Mexico and Central America. Other popular foods, like pizza, were brought to North America by immigrants.

North Americans love sports. In Mexico and neighboring countries, the top sport is soccer. In the United States, popular games include American football, basketball, and baseball.

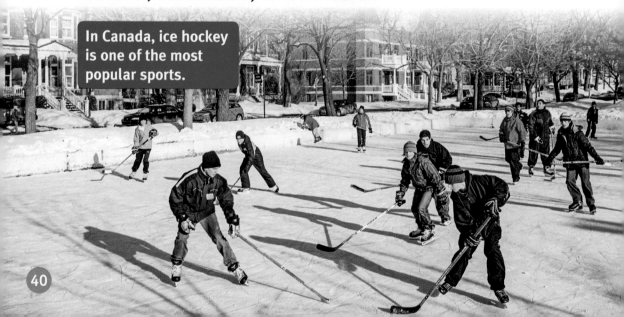

In Canada, ice hockey is one of the most popular sports.

The Day of the Dead is a special festival in Mexico. On that day, people remember their ancestors by dressing up and decorating cemeteries with bright flowers.

Celebrations

North America's calendar is full of colorful holidays. Every July 4, people in the United States light up the sky with fireworks to mark Independence Day. Other nations have similar days to celebrate their independence from colonial rule. Another celebration is Carnival. It takes place in late winter in many Caribbean and Central American countries. People dress in costumes and hold parades. ★

Chichén Itzá
Mexico

These Maya ruins include a pyramid that was used as a type of calendar! It has one step or platform for every day of the year.

Lake Atitlán
Guatemala

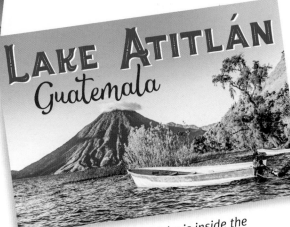

This beautiful lake is inside the crater of a volcano that erupted and collapsed 84,000 years ago.

L'Anse aux Meadows
Canada

This is the site of a 1,000-year-old Viking settlement. Experts have reconstructed the buildings.

Northern Lights
Arctic

When particles from the sun enter Earth's atmosphere in the Arctic, they create these colorful lights in the sky.

orth America

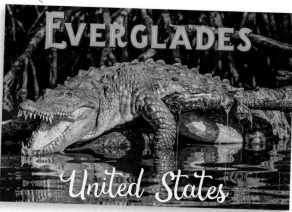

EVERGLADES
United States

This wetlands area is home to many amazing species, including the American crocodile.

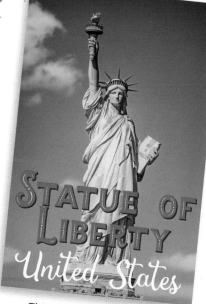

STATUE OF LIBERTY
United States

This statue is a symbol of American freedom. Millions of immigrants saw it when they sailed into New York Harbor.

YELLOWSTONE NATIONAL PARK
United States

This park in the western United States is known for its geysers. They are spots where hot water and steam burst out of the ground.

PANAMA CANAL
Panama

People created this waterway by digging away land. It is a shortcut for ships traveling between the Atlantic and Pacific Oceans.

Area of Greenland, the biggest island in the world: 836,300 sq. mi. (2,166,007 sq km)

Number of seats in Michigan Stadium, the continent's largest sports arena: 107,601

Total length of Canada's coast, the longest coastline on the planet: 125,566 mi. (202,080 km)

Length of Mammoth Cave in Kentucky, the world's biggest cave: 400 mi. (644 km)

Height of Denali, North America's tallest mountain: 20,310 ft. (6,190 m)

Number of tornadoes that strike each year in the United States, the world's busiest twister site: About 1,000

Maximum depth of Great Slave Lake in Canada, the deepest lake in North America: 2,015 ft. (614 m)

Did you find the truth?

 F Christopher Columbus was the first person from Europe to land in North America.

T In the northernmost parts of North America, no trees grow.

Resources

Books

Koenig, Emily. *North America*. Mankato, MN: ABDO Publishing, 2014.

Mann, Charles C. *Before Columbus: The Americas of 1491*. Austin, TX: Holt McDougal, 2009.

McDonnell, Ginger. *Next Stop: Mexico*. Huntington Beach, CA: Teacher Created Materials, 2011.

National Geographic Kids United States Atlas. Washington, D.C.: National Geographic, 2017.

Sexton, Colleen. *Canada*. Hopkins, MN: Bellwether Media, 2010.

Visit this Scholastic website for more information on North America:
★ www.factsfornow.scholastic.com
Enter the keywords **North America**

Important Words

climate (KLYE-mit) the usual weather in a place

colonies (KOL-uh-neez) territories that have been settled by people from another country and are controlled by that country

deciduous (dih-SIJ-oo-uhss) having to do with trees that shed their leaves every year

equator (ih-KWAY-tur) an imaginary line around the middle of Earth that is an equal distance from the North and South Poles

hibernate (HYE-bur-nate) to survive the winter in a type of deep sleep

immigrate (IM-uh-grayt) to go to a new country and settle there permanently

nomadic (noh-MAD-ik) wandering around instead of living in one place

predators (PRED-uh-turz) animals that live by hunting other animals for food

temperate (TEM-pur-it) having neither very high nor very low temperatures

tundra (TUHN-druh) a cold area of northern Europe, Asia, or North America where there are no trees and the soil under the surface of the ground is permanently frozen

Index

Page numbers in **bold** indicate illustrations.

About the Author

Karen Kellaher is an editor in Scholastic's classroom magazine division and has written more than 20 books for kids and teachers. She holds a bachelor's degree in communications from the University of Scranton (Pennsylvania) and a master's degree combining elementary education and publishing from New York University's Gallatin School of Individualized Study.